BEAR FAIRY EDUCATION

Sightword Top 100+ Words Reading & Writing Activity book for Grades 1 and 2

Published by: BEAR FAIRY EDUCATION.
Interior Design by: Pani Palmer, Kentucky
Cover Design by: Pani Palmer, Kentucky

10 9 8 7 6 5 4 3 2 1
1. Workbook for Kids 2. Basic Early Learning Children Book
First Edition

Sight word Set#1

Read and trace

and  be in

Find and circle

and	a	at	and	an
be	bee	bus	be	bet
in	in	inn	on	in

Find and Draw.

and
be
in
And
Be
In

q	w	e	A	n	d
r	a	n	d	t	y
u	i	o	p	a	s
B	e	d	g	h	j
k	l	z	b	e	x
c	v	b	n	m	m
i	n	q	w	I	n

cat and dog

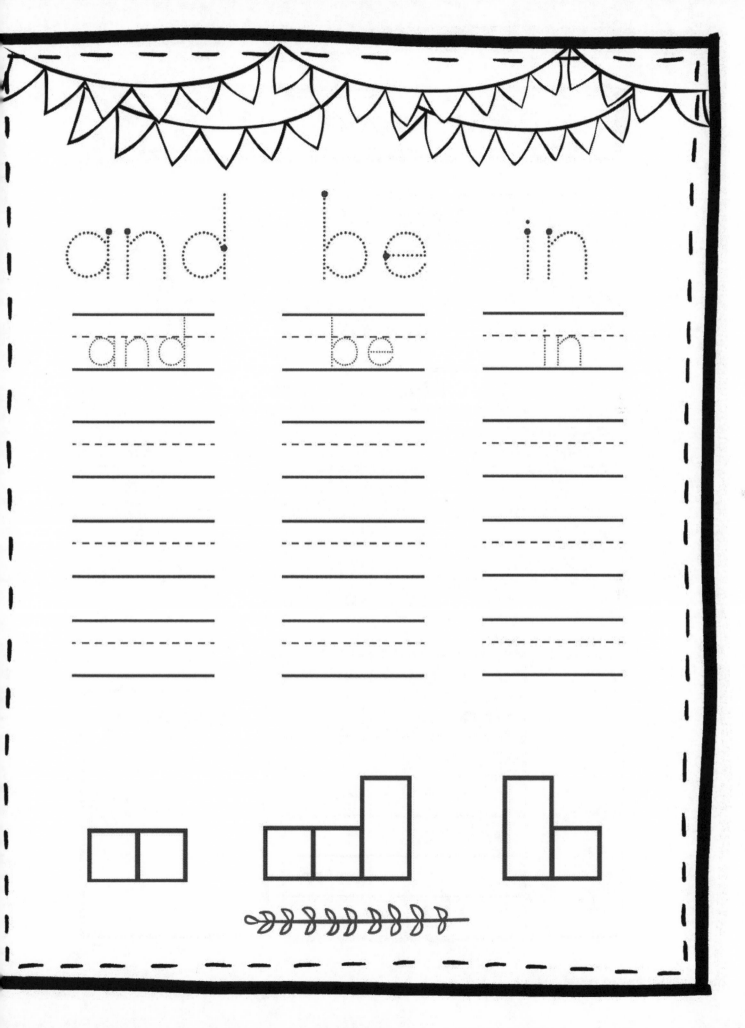

Sight word Set#2

is   it   of

Find and circle

is	it	sit	is	Is
it	to	it	sit	It
of	off	for	on	of

Find and Draw.

is
it
of
Is
It
Of

i	s	q	w	e	r
t	y	u	i	i	t
o	p	a	s	d	g
h	o	f	k	O	f
l	z	x	c	v	b
n	m	q	I	s	w
r	I	t	t	y	j

This is me.

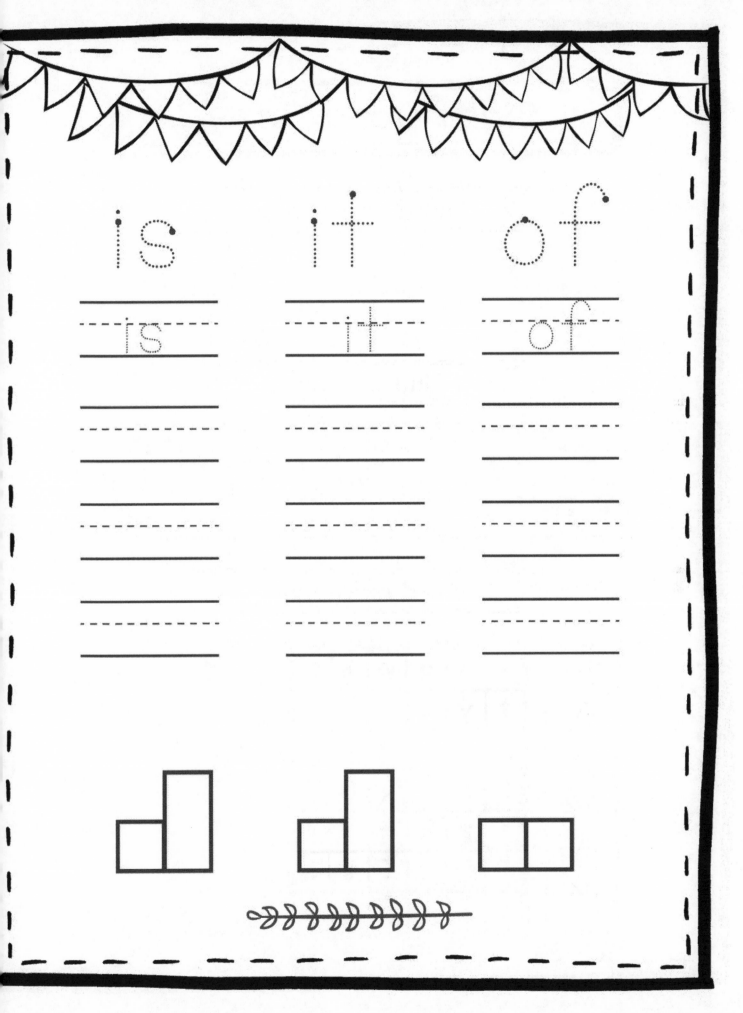

6-28-19

Sight word Set#3

Read and trace

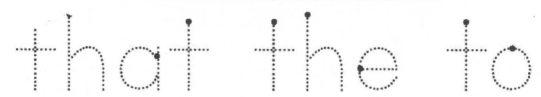

that the to

Find and circle

that	the	they	that	hat
the	them	the	they	They
to	too	two	got	to

Find and Draw.

that
the
to
That
The
To

q	t	h	a	t	w
t	o	e	r	t	t
y	u	i	o	p	a
s	d	d	t	h	e
T	h	a	t	f	g
h	j	k	T	h	e
T	o	l	z	x	c

Sit on the mat.

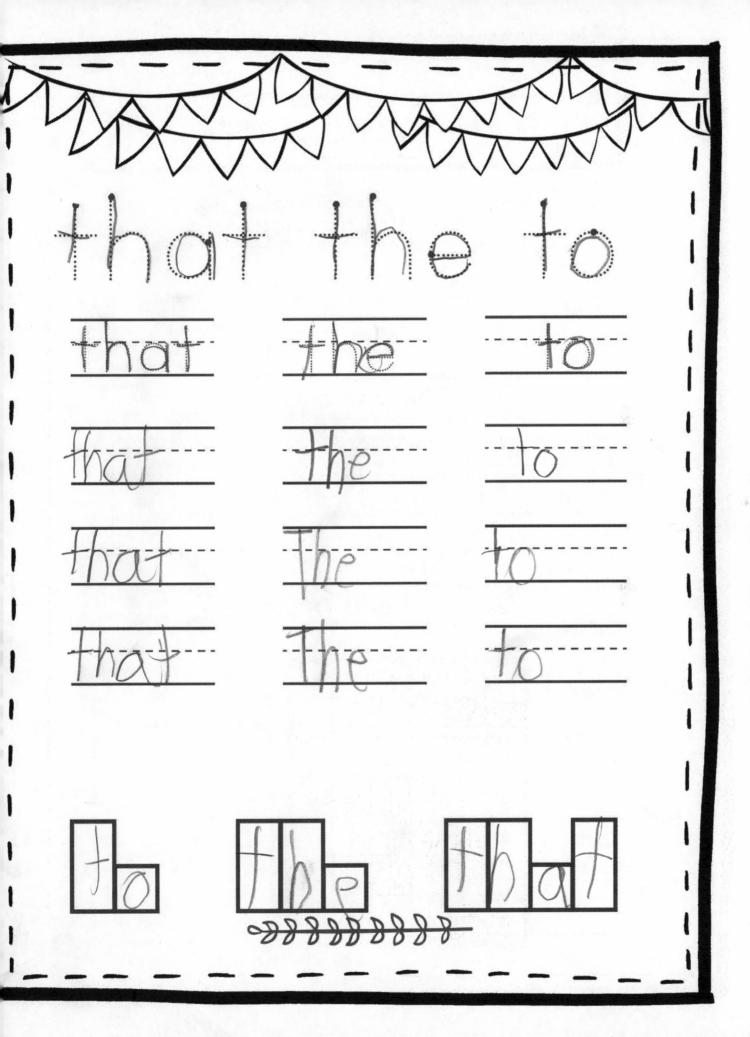

that the to

that   the   to

that   the   to

that   The   to

that   the   to

to   the   that

Sight word Set#4

Read and trace

was all as

Find and circle

was	as	was	saw	way
all	at	wall	all	All
as	as	As	am	at

Find and Draw.

was
all
as
Was
All
As

m	A	s	n	b	v
c	x	z	W	a	s
l	k	j	h	g	d
s	a	p	a	l	l
A	l	l	o	i	u
y	t	r	e	a	s
w	a	s	w	q	r

I was at school.

was   all   as

was   all   as

Sight word Set#5

Read and trace

are at but

Find and circle

are	as	am	are	Are
at	at	am	an	as
but	But	bud	but	hut

Find and Draw.

are
at
but
Are
At
But

a	r	e	z	x	c
v	b	n	b	u	t
m	a	t	h	j	k
l	q	w	e	r	y
u	i	A	r	e	o
A	t	p	a	s	d
f	g	B	u	t	h

I am at home.

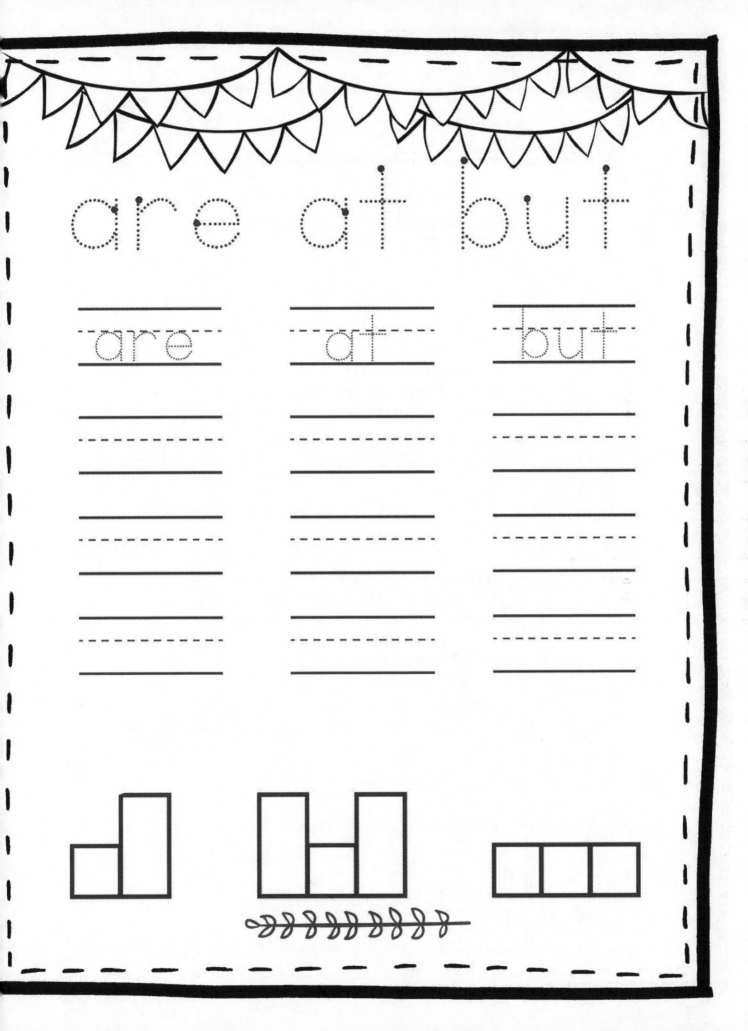

are at but

are   at   but

Sight word Set#6

Read and trace

for he her

Find and circle

for	from	for	or	For
he	him	her	He	he
her	herd	him	here	her

Find and Draw.

for
he
her
For
He
Her

x	c	v	h	e	m
h	f	o	r	y	k
d	r	y	u	i	s
w	h	e	r	t	y
a	s	d	g	H	e
F	o	r	h	m	b
f	m	x	H	e	r

Look at her.

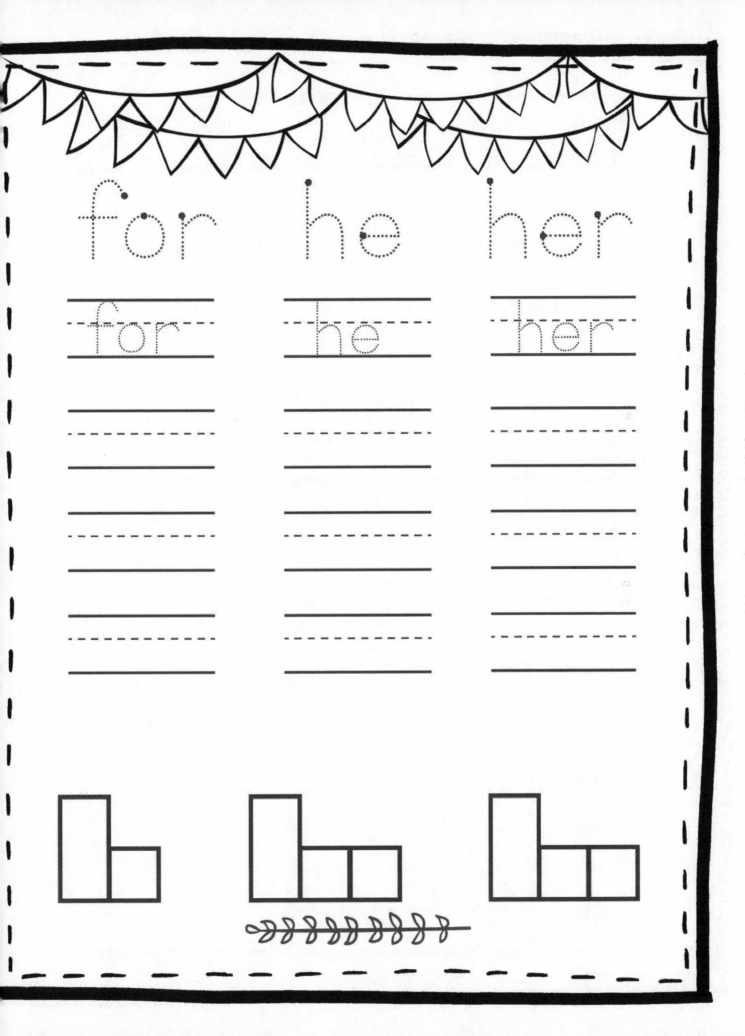

Sight word Set#7

Read and trace

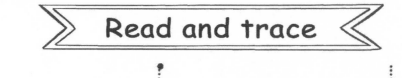

Find and circle

an	a	at	and	an
by	by	bus	be	bet
do	did	does	do	Do

Find and Draw.

an
by
do
An
By
Do

q	w	e	r	B	y
t	a	n	y	u	i
o	p	a	D	o	s
d	f	g	h	j	k
l	z	x	A	n	c
b	y	v	b	n	m
n	b	v	c	d	o

an apple

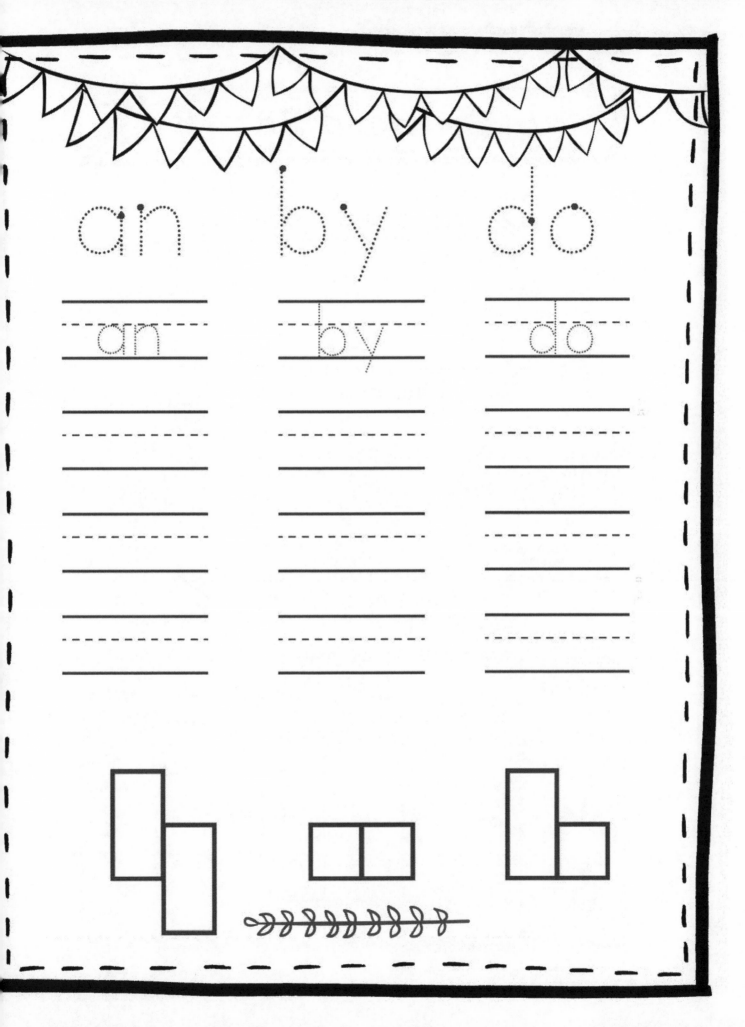

an by do

an by do

Sight word Set#8

Read and trace

go had have

Find and circle

go	got	gone	go	Go
had	hat	bad	had	have
have	have	hand	hold	has

Find and Draw.

go
had
have
Go
Had
Have

m	g	o	n	b	v
c	x	z	l	k	j
h	g	h	a	v	e
f	d	s	G	o	s
H	a	v	e	a	p
o	h	a	d	i	u
y	t	r	H	a	d

Go to school!

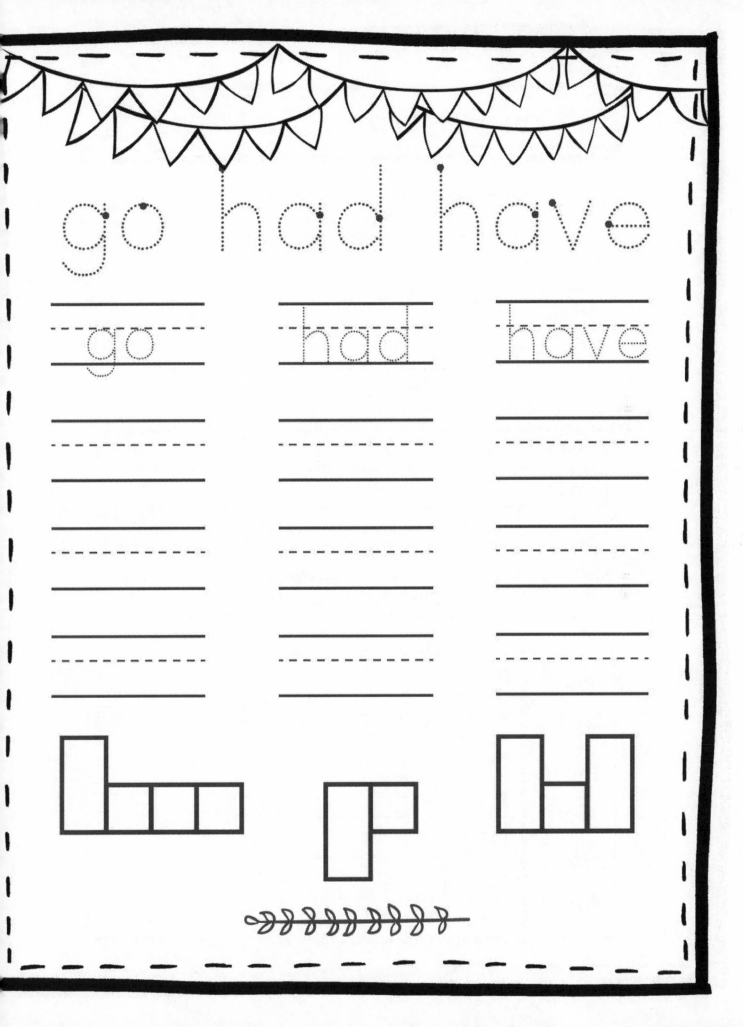

go had have

go   had   have

Sight word Set#9

Read and trace

his if me

Find and circle

his	this	hill	his	her
if	If	if	of	it
me	my	met	me	Me

Find and Draw.

his
if
me
His
If
Me

h	i	s	q	i	f
w	e	r	t	y	u
m	e	i	o	M	e
p	a	s	d	f	g
h	j	k	H	i	s
l	z	x	c	v	b
I	f	b	n	m	m

Look at me.

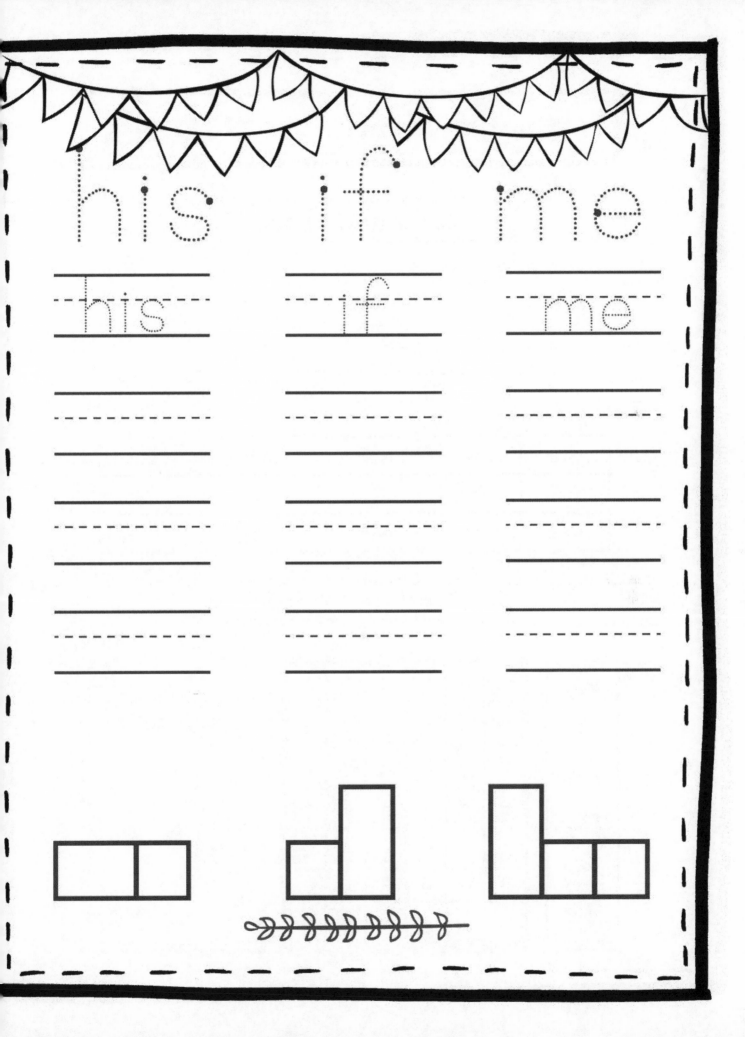

his   if   me

his   if   me

Sight word Set#10

my   no   not

Find and circle

my	me	my	My	mum
no	not	now	no	No
not	no	Not	net	not

Find and Draw.

my
no
not
My
No
Not

m	n	b	v	n	o
c	m	y	x	z	l
k	j	h	g	f	d
s	a	n	o	t	p
o	i	u	y	M	y
t	N	o	r	e	w
q	w	e	N	o	t

Look at my dog.

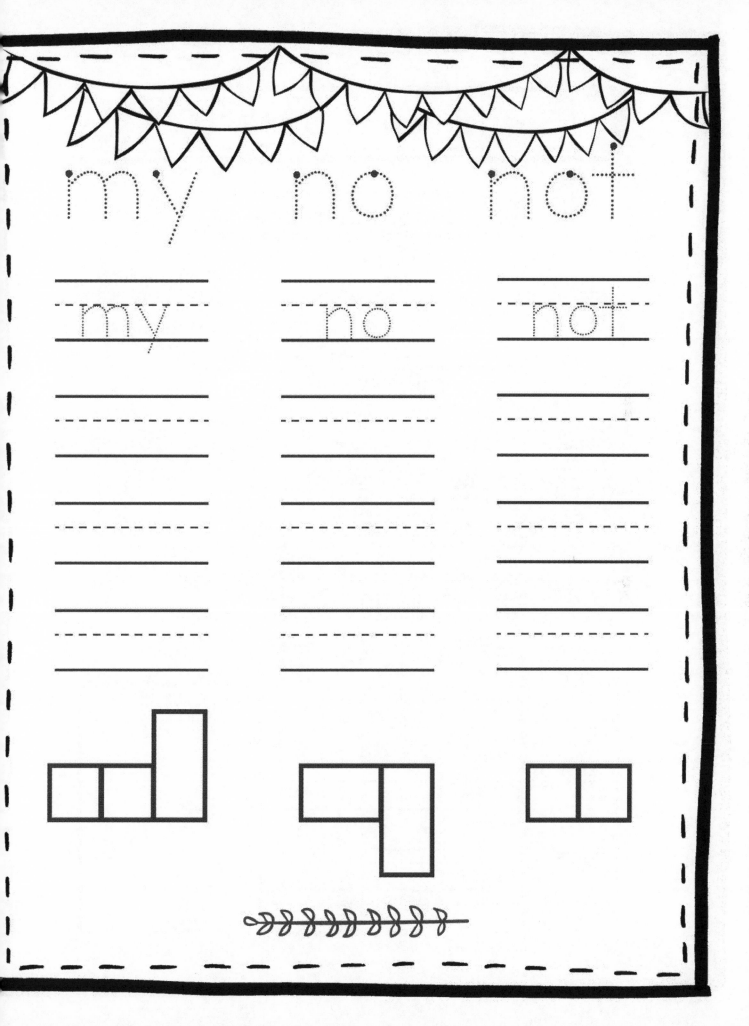

my   no   not

Sight word Set#11

Read and trace

on one said

Find and circle

on	one	One	on	On
one	One	on	one	On
said	say	aid	Said	said

Find and Draw.

| on |
| one |
| said |
| On |
| One |
| Said |

q	w	e	o	n	r
s	a	i	d	t	y
i	O	n	o	p	a
s	d	S	a	i	d
O	n	e	f	g	h
j	k	l	o	n	e
z	x	c	v	b	n

one cat

Sight word Set#12

Read and trace

so   we   you

Find and circle

so	see	so	was	set
we	when	We	we	wet
you	your	why	you	Your

Find and Draw.

so						
we	S	o	m	n	b	v
you	c	x	z	s	o	l
So	q	a	Y	o	u	k
We	w	e	s	d	d	j
You	b	e	r	f	g	h
	t	y	u	y	o	u
	i	W	e	o	p	t

We are at school.

so   we   you

so   we   you

Sight word Set#13

Read and trace

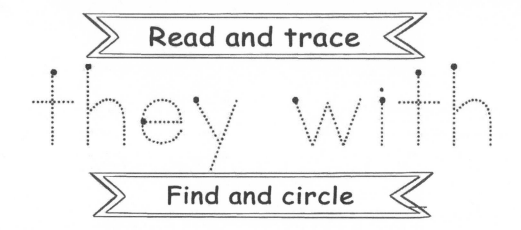

Find and circle

they	They	them	there	they
with	will	With	with	won't

Find and Draw.

they
with
They
With

q	a	z	w	s	x
e	d	t	h	e	y
W	i	t	h	c	r
f	v	t	g	b	y
h	T	h	e	y	n
u	j	m	i	k	l
o	p	w	i	t	h

I am with Dad.

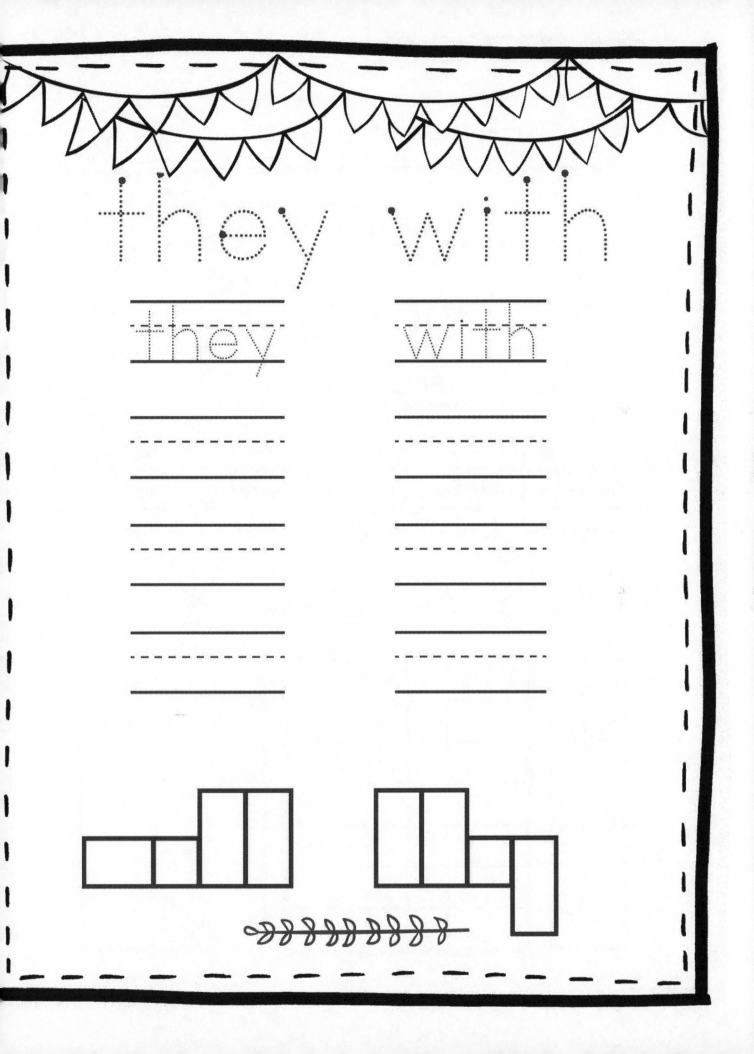

they with

they with

Sight word Set#14

back who has

Find and circle

back	band	deck	back	ball
who	went	you	why	who
has	had	has	hat	ham

Find and Draw.

back
has
who
Back
Has
Who

b	a	c	k	q	w
e	w	h	o	r	t
y	u	i	h	a	s
o	p	a	s	d	f
g	h	B	a	c	k
H	a	s	j	k	l
z	x	c	W	h	o

Dad has a hat on.

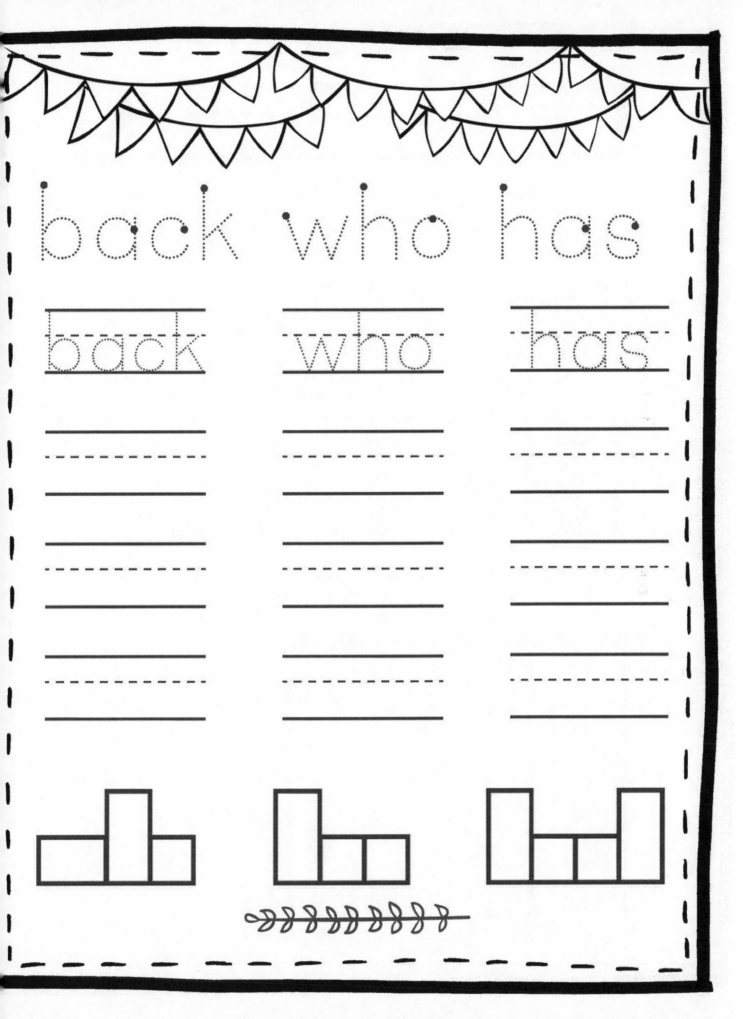

Sight word Set#15

Read and trace

big off she

Find and circle

big	pig	wig	big	dig
off	of	off	on	Off
she	she	he	see	shed

Find and Draw.

big
off
she
Big
Off
She

m	n	b	O	f	f
v	b	i	g	c	x
z	l	k	g	h	g
B	i	g	d	s	a
q	w	e	r	t	y
s	h	e	o	f	f
y	i	S	h	e	p

Here is a big dog.

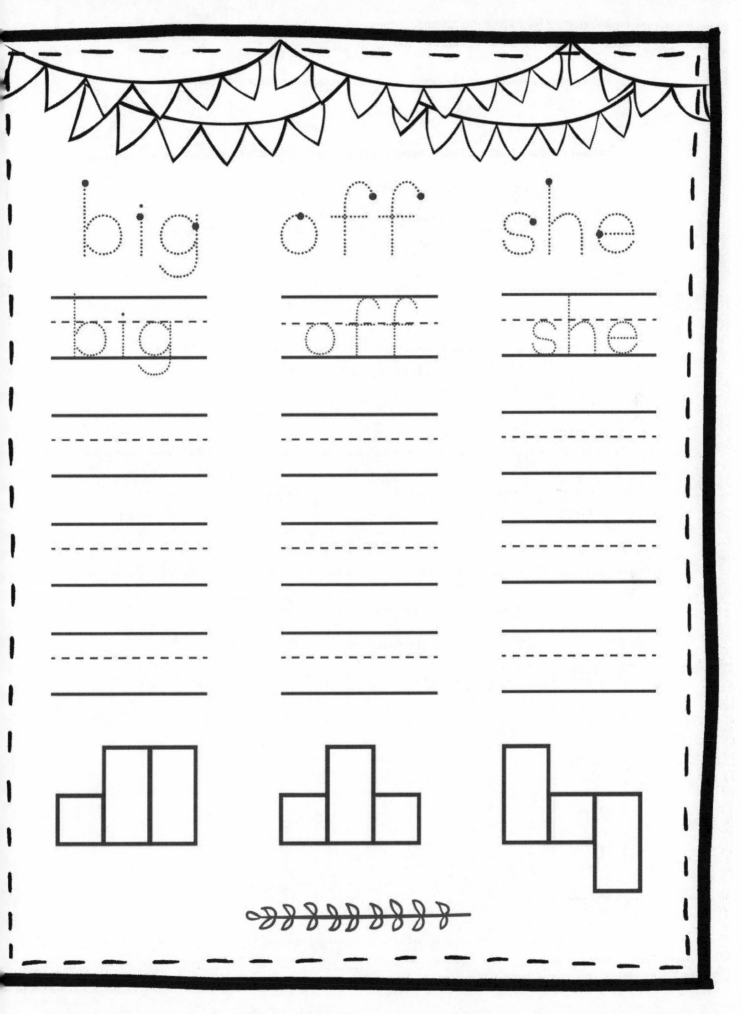

Sight word Set#16

Read and trace

him new out

Find and circle

him	him	her	dim	Him
new	men	net	new	New
out	our	old	Out	out

Find and Draw.

him
new
out
Him
New
Out

m	n	b	o	u	t
v	h	i	m	c	x
n	e	w	z	l	k
h	g	N	e	w	f
d	s	a	H	i	m
q	w	e	r	t	y
O	u	t	y	i	o

I have a new hat.

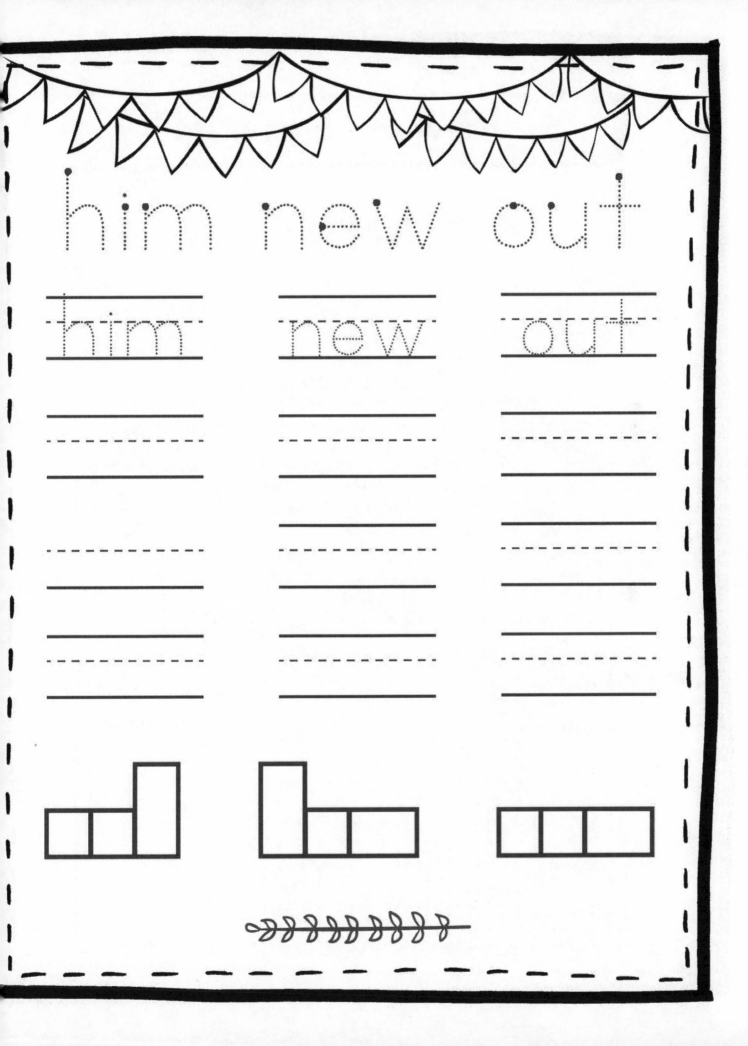

him new out

him new out

Sight word Set#17

Read and trace

get now two

Find and circle

get	got	Get	jet	get
now	new	not	Not	now
two	too	Too	two	to

Find and Draw.

get
now
two
Get
Now
Two

q	g	e	t	w	e
r	t	n	o	w	y
T	w	o	i	o	p
a	s	d	f	g	h
N	o	w	G	e	t
k	l	z	x	c	b
n	m	y	t	w	o

I have two eyes.

get now two

get now two

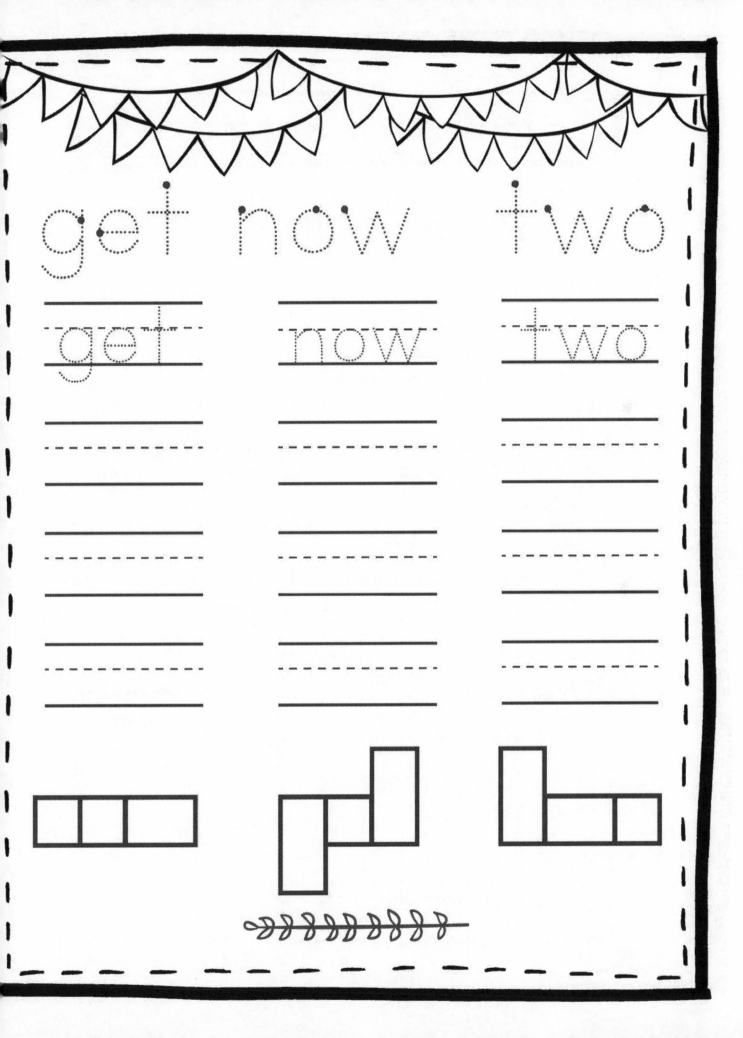

Sight word Set#18

Read and trace

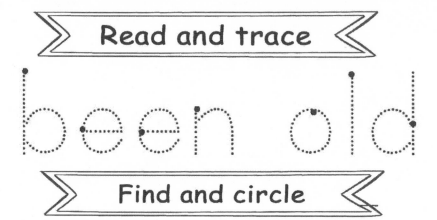

been old

Find and circle

been	bean	beans	been	Bee
old	cold	Old	old	owl

Find and Draw.

been
old
Been
Old

q	a	z	w	s	x
e	b	e	e	n	d
c	r	f	o	l	d
v	t	g	b	y	h
n	u	B	e	e	n
j	m	i	k	o	l
O	l	d	p	q	a

This man is old.

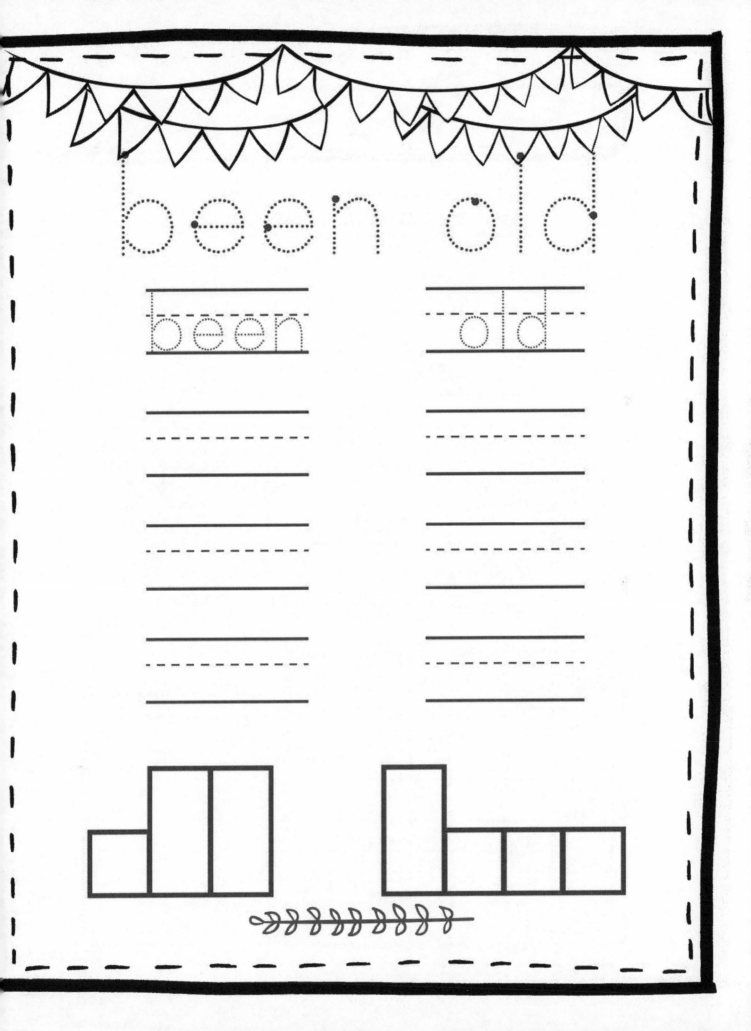

Sight word Set#19

Read and trace

call   like   this

Find and circle

call	hall	cell	call	well
like	Like	lime	like	look
this	this	them	then	This

Find and Draw.

call
like
this
Call
Like
This

q	w	c	a	l	l
e	l	i	k	e	r
t	y	L	i	k	e
C	a	l	l	y	i
g	t	h	i	s	o
T	h	i	s	p	a
r	k	m	b	f	d

I like school.

call like this

call like this

Sight word Set#20

Read and trace

came only well

Find and circle

came	came	come	cane	Came
only	Only	only	one	old
well	went	we	Well	well

Find and Draw.

came
only
well
Came
Only
Well

q	a	o	n	l	y
z	c	a	m	e	w
e	d	w	e	l	l
C	a	m	e	c	v
r	f	v	t	g	b
y	O	n	l	y	g
k	p	W	e	l	l

I came to school.

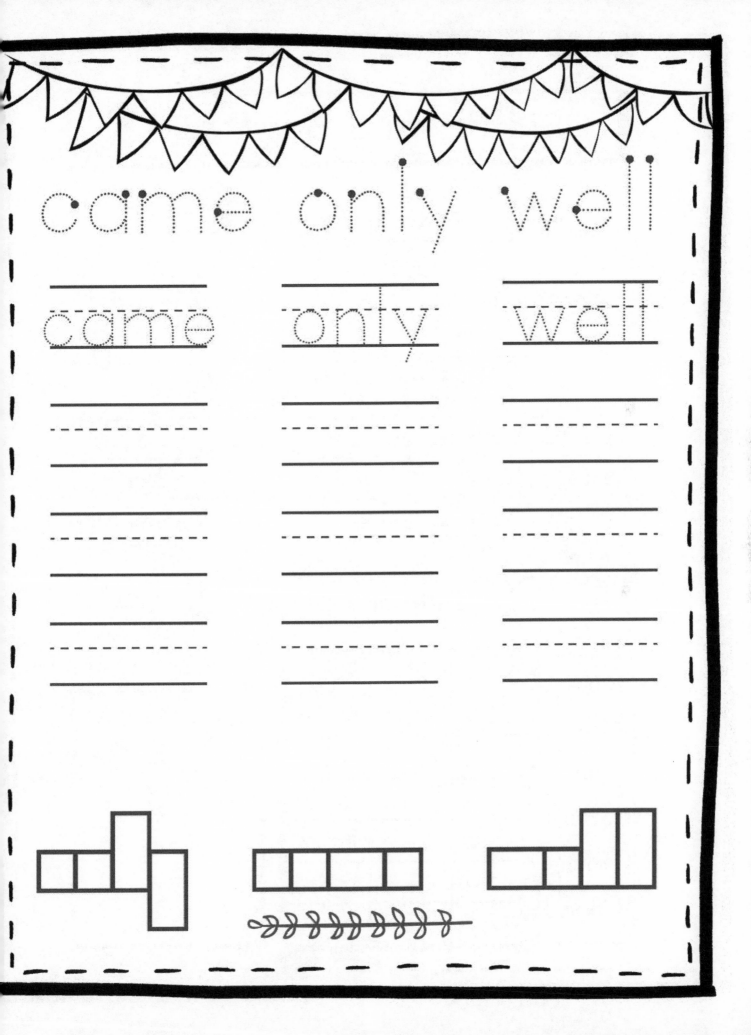

came only well

came only well

Sight word Set#21

Read and trace

come over when

Find and circle

come	came	come	cane	Came
over	over	old	of	or
when	where	When	when	who

Find and Draw.

come
over
when
Come
Over
When

o	v	e	r	v	g
q	e	c	o	m	e
a	w	h	e	n	y
z	C	o	m	e	b
w	d	r	f	t	h
s	O	v	e	r	n
x	c	W	h	e	n

Come to me.

come over when

come over when

_____
_____

_____
_____

_____
_____

_____
_____

_____
_____

Sight word Set#22

Read and trace

down made went

Find and circle

down	down	town	Down	own
made	make	made	Made	must
went	when	wet	went	who

Find and Draw.

down
made
went
Down
Made
Went

q	z	m	a	d	e
a	d	o	w	n	c
w	s	y	e	d	r
D	o	w	n	v	f
y	h	w	e	n	t
n	M	a	d	e	t
W	e	n	t	b	g

I went home.

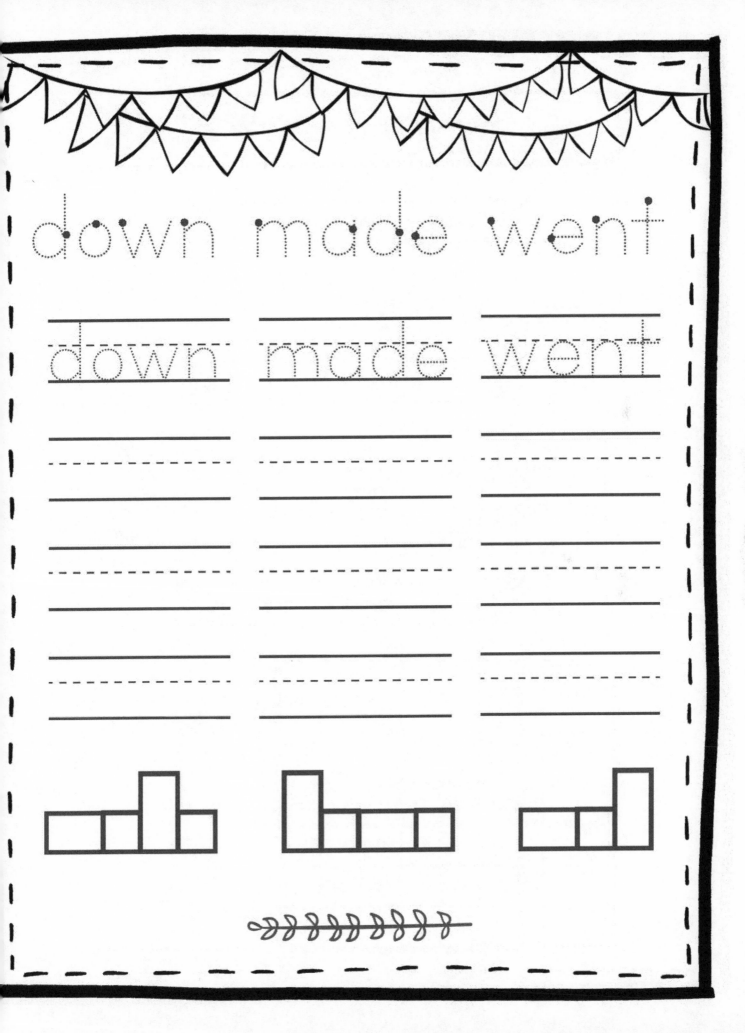

down made went

down made went

Sight word Set#23

Read and trace

can or up

Find and circle

can	can	man	cap	cat
or	Or	old	of	or
up	Up	up	us	pup

Find and Draw.

can
or
up
Can
Or
Up

c	q	w	e	r	t
u	i	o	C	a	n
p	c	a	n	a	s
u	p	d	f	O	r
g	h	j	k	l	l
c	o	r	v	b	n
e	t	y	u	U	p

I can run.

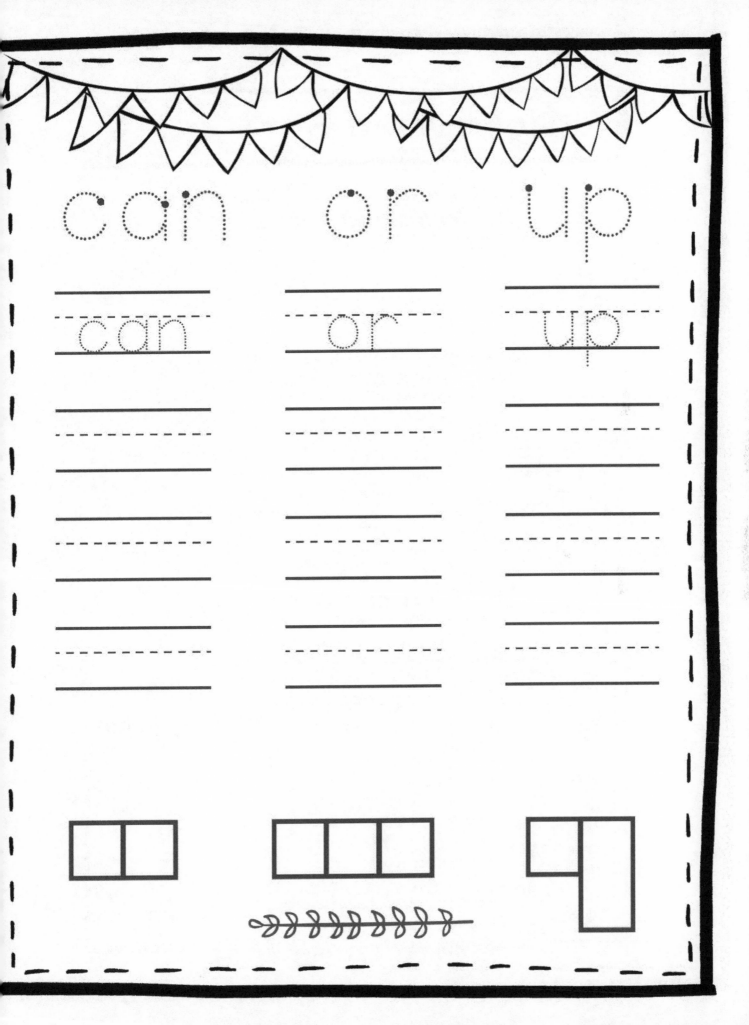

can   or   up

can   or   up

Sight word Set#24

Read and trace

did   our   see

Find and circle

did	Did	pip	did	dad
our	out	own	our	Our
see	she	set	sea	see

Find and Draw.

did
our
see
Did
Our
See

d	i	d	f	g	h
e	r	t	S	e	e
o	u	r	o	o	d
d	b	v	e	w	e
s	e	e	D	i	d
m	k	s	a	s	x
O	u	r	q	e	n

See me jump.

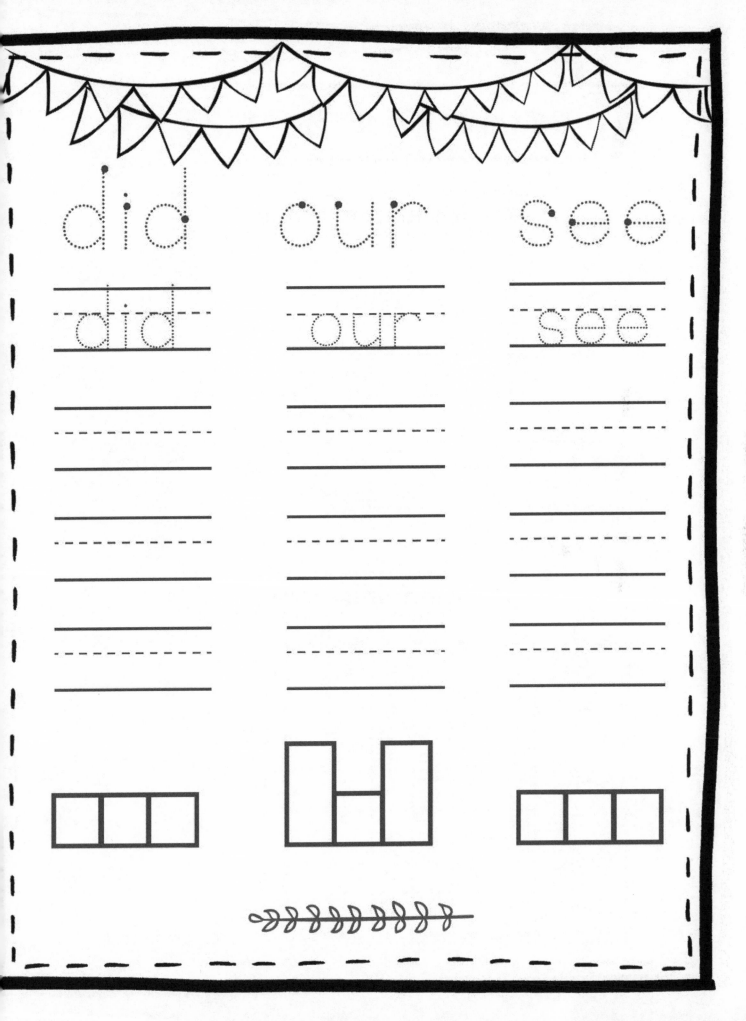

Sight word Set# 25

Read and trace

before there

Find and circle

before	become	for	before	Before
there	their	there	them	then

Find and Draw.

before
there
Before
There

p	o	i	y	t	r
b	e	f	o	r	e
e	w	q	l	k	h
g	t	h	e	r	e
f	d	s	a	a	m
B	e	f	o	r	e
n	T	h	e	r	e

A cat is over there.

before there

before   there

Sight word Set# 26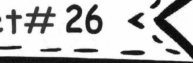

Read and trace

about will then

Find and circle

about	boat	out	about	About
will	Will	hill	mill	will
then	this	them	then	Then

Find and Draw.

about
will
then
About
Will
Then

z	x	w	i	l	l
v	n	T	h	e	n
q	t	h	e	n	h
W	i	l	l	t	y
a	s	d	f	g	h
n	A	b	o	u	t
a	b	o	u	t	m

I will go home.

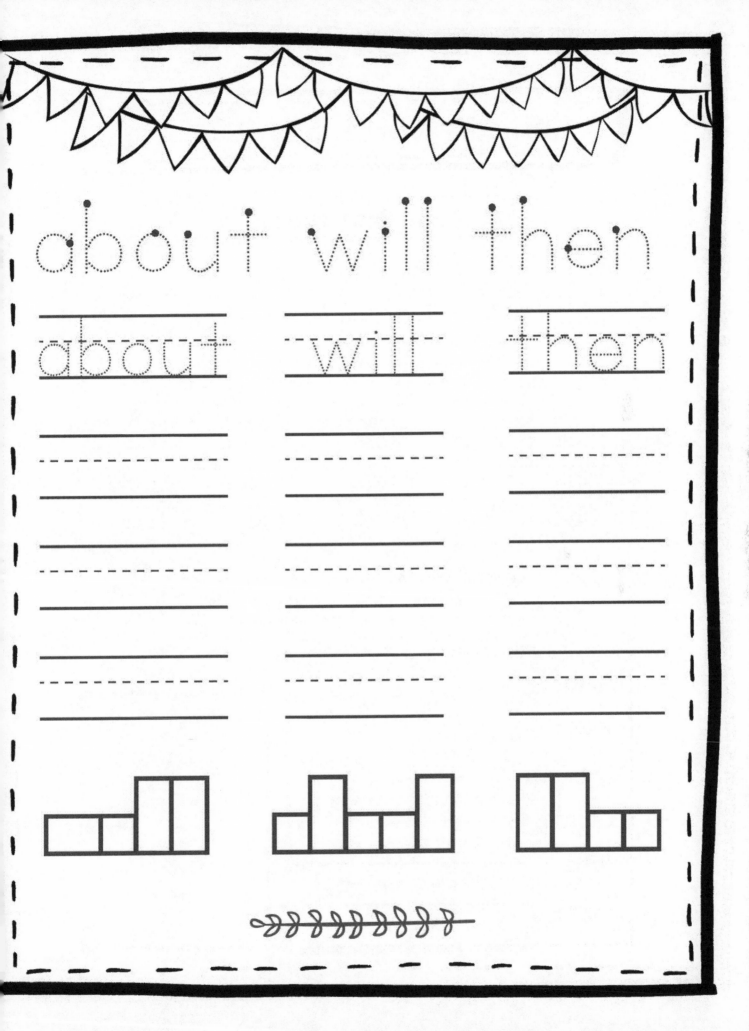

Sight word Set#27

Read and trace

from make them

Find and circle

from	for	from	From	four
make	made	mate	make	Made
them	they	then	them	Them

Find and Draw.

from	q	f	r	o	m	w
make	M	a	k	e	e	r
them	t	y	t	h	e	m
From	u	F	r	o	m	i
Make	o	p	a	s	d	f
Them	T	h	e	m	g	h
	j	k	m	a	k	e

Look at them.

from make them

from make them

Sight word Set#28

Read and trace

here   much   into

Find and circle

here	here	Here	hair	her
much	Much	much	mush	made
into	too	in	into	to

Find and Draw.

here
much
into
Here
Much
Into

q	i	n	t	o	w
M	u	c	h	e	r
t	y	h	e	r	e
i	o	p	a	s	d
f	H	e	r	e	g
h	k	I	n	t	o
m	u	c	h	l	z

The cat is here.

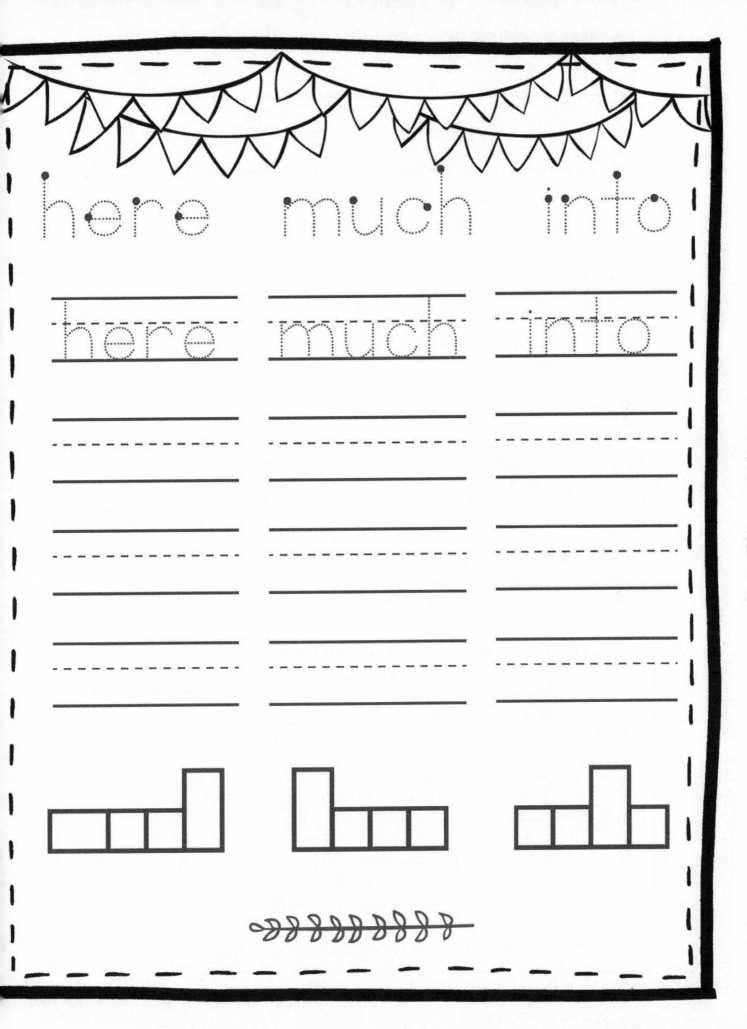

here   much   into

here   much   into

Sight word Set#29

Read and trace

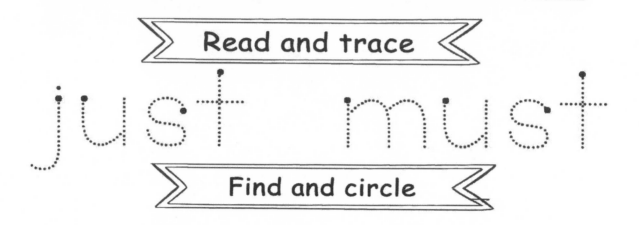

Find and circle

just	juice	Just	must	just
must	must	Must	just	Just

Find and Draw.

just
must
Just
Must

q	j	u	s	t	z
a	w	s	z	e	d
c	J	u	s	t	r
f	v	t	g	b	y
h	n	m	u	s	t
m	k	l	p	o	i
M	u	s	t	y	t

You must stop here.

just   must

just   must

Sight word Set# 30

Read and trace

your their little

Find and circle

your	you	you're	Your	your
their	then	their	there	this
little	kettle	Little	little	Little

Find and Draw.

your
their
little
Your
Their
Little

L	i	t	t	l	e
q	w	e	r	t	y
y	o	u	r	f	g
t	h	e	i	r	k
m	Y	o	u	r	n
T	h	e	i	r	l
l	i	t	t	l	e

the little dog

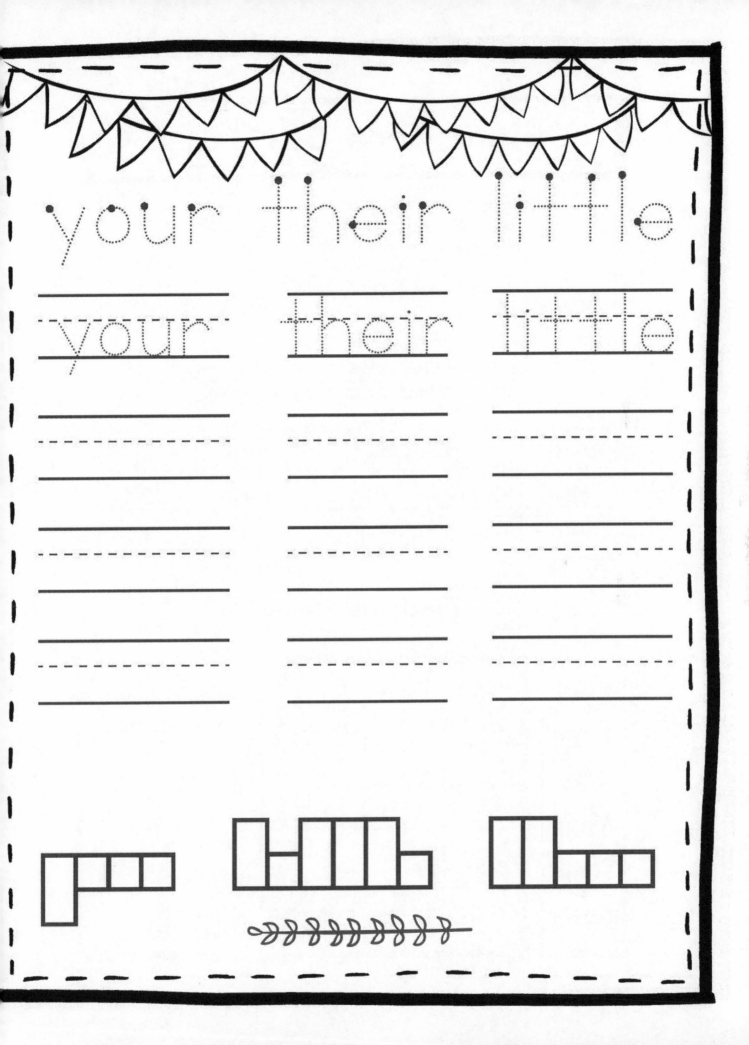

your their little

your   their   little

Sight word Set# 31

Read and trace

what some look

Find and circle

what	when	where	what	What
some	home	some	sole	Some
look	Look	book	look	leek

Find and Draw.

what
some
look
What
Some
Look

a	w	h	a	t	q
S	o	m	e	w	e
l	o	o	k	g	h
e	f	h	i	g	h
t	f	L	o	o	k
v	s	o	m	e	t
c	W	h	a	t	k

Look at me.

what some look

what   some   look

Sight word Set# 32

Read and trace

which want more

Find and circle

which	witch	which	when	where
want	want	went	plant	Want
more	mere	more	More	pore

Find and Draw.

which
want
more
Which
Want
More

w	a	n	t	d	r
a	s	d	f	g	h
k	w	h	i	c	h
W	h	i	c	h	k
e	e	M	o	r	e
W	a	n	t	e	r
h	l	m	o	r	e

I want a toy.

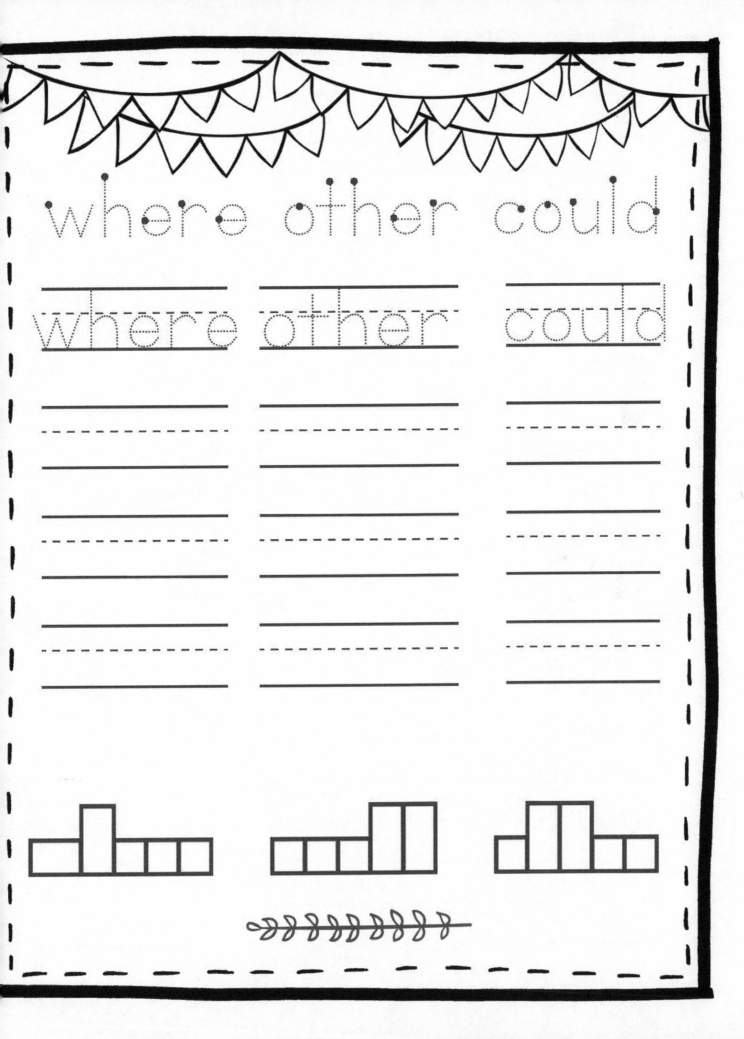

where other could

where other could

Made in the USA
San Bernardino, CA
25 June 2019